PUFFIN BOOKS
Editor: Kaye

FIGGIE HOBBIN

POETRY FOR CHILDREN

Figgie hobbin is a light, Cornish pudding or plum duff, creamy-white in colour and sweetened with raisins, which are called 'figs' in Cornwall. It can be eaten with meat as a savoury, or (with the addition of more raisins) as a sweet, with Cornish cream or custard.

Charles Causley's *Figgie Hobbin*, one of the most popular and well-loved collections of poems for children to have been published in the last decade, is also firmly Cornish in flavour, and sometimes savoury and sometimes sweet. Here we meet many celebrated characters: Colonel Fazackerley, who was unlucky enough to buy an old castle complete with a ghost; Mr Pennycomequick, who jumped off the top of Launceston Castle using a carriage-umbrella as a parachute; Old Mrs Thing-um-e-bob; and the famous Jolly Hunter with his jolly gun.

The poems range from the nonsensical near nursery rhyming of *'Quack!' said the billy-goat* and *As I went down Zig Zag* to the haunting ballad strain of *Mary, Mary Magdalene* and the lyrical beauty and intensity of such poems as *My mother saw a dancing bear*, *Tom Bone* and *Who?*

As the King in the title poem remarks, 'To cure the sickness of the heart, ah – bring me some figgie hobbin!' Here is a feast indeed.

FIGGIE HOBBIN

by
Charles Causley

Illustrated by Jill Bennett

PUFFIN BOOKS

Puffin Books,
Penguin Books Ltd, Harmondsworth,
Middlesex, England
Penguin Books, 625 Madison Avenue,
New York, New York 10022, U.S.A.
Penguin Books Australia Ltd, Ringwood,
Victoria, Australia
Penguin Books Canada Ltd, 2801 John Street,
Markham, Ontario, Canada L3R 1B4
Penguin Books (N.Z.) Ltd, 182–190 Wairau Road,
Auckland 10, New Zealand

First published by Macmillan London Ltd 1970
Published in Puffin Books 1979
Copyright © Charles Causley, 1970
Illustrations copyright © Jill Bennett, 1979
All rights reserved

Made and printed in Great Britain by
Richard Clay (The Chaucer Press) Ltd
Bungay, Suffolk
Set in Monophoto Baskerville

CONTENTS

Figgie hobbin is a Cornish pudding, sweetened with raisins, which are known as 'figs' in Cornwall. It may be eaten either with meat, or (with the addition of more raisins) as a sweet.

To Cynthia and Stanley Simmonds

EAGLE ONE, EAGLE TWO

Eagle one, eagle two,
Standing on the wall,
Your wings a-spread are made of lead,
You never fly at all.

High on the roof, Britannia
Holds her fishing-prong,
And she and they as white as clay
Stand still the whole day long.

And one looks to the eastward,
One to the setting sun,
And one looks down upon the town
Until the day is done.

But when the Quarterjacks their twelve
Upon the black town beat,
And when the moon's a gold balloon
Blowing down Castle Street,

Then with her spear, Britannia
The eagles both will guide
To drink their fill under the hill
Down by the riverside.

And when the Town Hall Quarterjacks
The hour of one beat plain,
Eagles and queen may all be seen
On wall and roof again.

But now I am a grown man
And hear the midnight bell,
Ask, is it true, the tale I knew
That still the children tell?

I only know at midnight
Softly I go by,
Nor look at all on roof and wall.
Do not ask me why.

RILEY

Down in the water-meadows Riley
Spread his wash on the bramble-thorn,
Sat, one foot in the moving water,
Bare as the day that he was born.

Candid was his curling whisker,
Brown his body as an old tree-limb,
Blue his eye as the jay above him
Watching him watch the minjies swim.   *small minnows*

Four stout sticks for walls had Riley,
His roof was a rusty piece of tin,
As snug in the lew of a Cornish hedgerow   *lee*
He watched the seasons out and in.

He paid no rates, he paid no taxes,
His lamp was the moon hung in the tree.
Though many an ache and pain had Riley
He envied neither you nor me.

Many a friend from bush or burrow
To Riley's hand would run or fly,
And soft he'd sing and sweet he'd whistle
Whatever the weather in the sky.

Till one winter's morning Riley
From the meadow vanished clean.
Gone was the rusty tin, the timber,
As if old Riley had never been.

What strange secret had old Riley?
Where did he come from? Where did he go?
Why was his heart as light as summer?
'Never know now,' said the jay. 'Never know.'

I SAW A JOLLY HUNTER

I saw a jolly hunter
  With a jolly gun
Walking in the country
  In the jolly sun.

In the jolly meadow
  Sat a jolly hare.
Saw the jolly hunter.
  Took jolly care.

Hunter jolly eager –
 Sight of jolly prey.
Forgot gun pointing
 Wrong jolly way.

Jolly hunter jolly head
 Over heels gone.
Jolly old safety-catch
 Not jolly on.

Bang went the jolly gun.
 Hunter jolly dead.
Jolly hare got clean away.
 Jolly good, I said.

WHAT HAS
HAPPENED TO LULU?

What has happened to Lulu, mother?
  What has happened to Lu?
There's nothing in her bed but an old rag-doll
  And by its side a shoe.

Why is her window wide, mother,
  The curtain flapping free,
And only a circle on the dusty shelf
  Where her money-box used to be?

Why do you turn your head, mother,
  And why do the tear-drops fall?
And why do you crumple that note on the fire
  And say it is nothing at all?

I woke to voices late last night,
  I heard an engine roar.
Why do you tell me the things I heard
  Were a dream and nothing more?

I heard somebody cry, mother,
  In anger or in pain,
But now I ask you why, mother,
  You say it was a gust of rain.

Why do you wander about as though
  You don't know what to do?
What has happened to Lulu, mother?
  What has happened to Lu?

A FOX CAME
INTO MY GARDEN

A fox came into my garden.
'What do you want from me?'
'Heigh-ho, Johnnie-boy,
A chicken for my tea.'

'Oh no, you beggar, and never, you thief,
My chicken you must leave,
That she may run and she may fly
From now to Christmas Eve.'

'What are you eating, Johnnie-boy,
Between two slices of bread?'
'I'm eating a piece of chicken-breast
And it's honey-sweet,' I said.

'Heigh-ho, you diddling man,
I thought that was what I could smell.
What, some for you and none for me?
Give us a piece as well!'

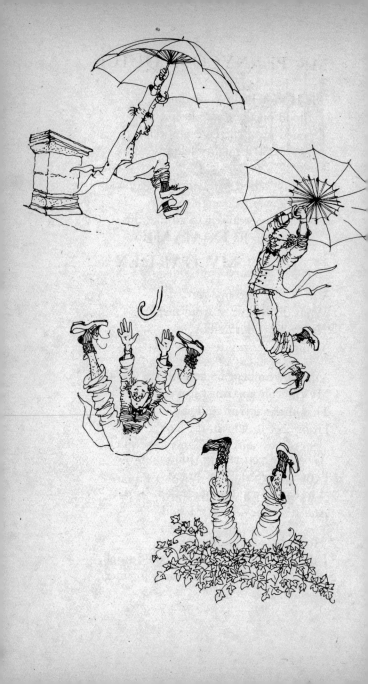

MR PENNYCOMEQUICK

Mr Hector Pennycomequick
    Stood on the castle keep,
Opened up a carriage-umbrella
    And took a mighty leap.

'Hooray!' cried Mr Pennycomequick
    As he went through the air.
'I've always wanted to go like this
    From here to Newport Square.'

But Mr Hector Pennycomequick
    He never did float nor fly.
He landed in an ivy-bush,
    His legs up in the sky.

Mr Hector Pennycomequick
    They hurried home to bed
With a bump the size of a sea-gull's egg
    On the top of his head.

'So sorry,' said Mr Pennycomequick,
    'For causing all this fuss.
When next I go to Newport Square
    I think I'll take the bus.'

The moral of this little tale
    Is difficult to refute:
A carriage-umbrella's a carriage-umbrella
    And not a parachute.

'QUACK!'
SAID THE BILLY-GOAT

'Quack!' said the billy-goat.
  'Oink!' said the hen.
'Miaow!' said the little chick
  Running in the pen.

'Hobble-gobble!' said the dog.
  'Cluck!' said the sow.
'Tu-whit tu-whoo!' the donkey said.
  'Baa!' said the cow.

'Hee-haw!' the turkey cried.
  The duck began to moo.
All at once the sheep went,
  'Cock-a-doodle-doo!'

The owl coughed and cleared his throat
  And he began to bleat.
'Bow-wow!' said the cock
  Swimming in the leat.

'Cheep-cheep!' said the cat
  As she began to fly.
'Farmer's been and laid an egg –
  That's the reason why.'

SALL SCRATCH

*When a Cornishwoman puts on
old clothes to do her house-work in,
she is said to look like 'Sall Scratch'.*

Sall Scratch
Wore her husband's cap
The dust and dirt to beat,
An apron of sack
And one on her back
And Wellingtons on her feet.

With bucket and mop
She'd hardly stop
For a cup of strong tea at eleven,
And in shine or slush
Her steps she'd brush
Till they looked like the path to heaven.

With verve and vim
Both out and in
For her home she'd lovingly care
From the front-door brass
To the panes of glass
In the skylight over the stair.

She'd have been quite a Turk
If when home from his work
Her husband came in through the door
Without putting his feet
On each newspaper sheet
Laid out on the kitchen floor.

You may think such a house
Over-clean for her spouse,
But there neither was sorrow nor strife,
For by dirt and by dust
He was equally fussed
And as good (or as bad) as his wife.

AS I WENT DOWN ZIG ZAG

*Zig Zag is the name of a steep
footpath in Launceston.*

As I went down Zig Zag
  The clock striking one,
I saw a man cooking
  An egg in the sun.

As I went down Zig Zag
  The clock striking two,
I watched a man walk
  With one boot and one shoe.

As I went down Zig Zag
  The clock striking three,
I heard a man murmuring
  'Buzz!' like a bee.

As I went down Zig Zag
  The clock striking four,
I saw a man swim
  In no sea by no shore.

As I went down Zig Zag
  The clock striking five,
I caught a man keeping
  A hog in a hive.

As I went down Zig Zag
  The clock striking six,
I met a man making
  A blanket of bricks.

As I went down Zig Zag
  The clock striking seven,
A man asked me if
  I was odd or was even.

As I went down Zig Zag
  The clock striking eight,
I saw a man sailing
  A seven-barred gate.

As I went down Zig Zag
  The clock striking nine,
I saw a man milking
  Where never were kine.

As I went down Zig Zag
  The clock striking ten,
I watched a man waltz
  With a cock and a hen.

As I went down Zig Zag
  The clock striking eleven,
I saw a man baking
  A loaf with no leaven.

As I went down Zig Zag
  The clock striking twelve,
For dyes from the rainbow
  I saw a man delve.

So if you'd keep your senses,
  The point of my rhyme
Is don't go down Zig Zag
  When the clocks start to chime.

FIGGIE HOBBIN

Nightingales' tongues, your majesty?
  Quails in aspic, cost a purse of money?
Oysters from the deep, raving sea?
  Grapes and Greek honey?
Beads of black caviare from the Caspian?
  Rock melon with corn on the cob in?
Take it all away! grumbled the old King of Cornwall.
  Bring me some figgie hobbin!

Devilled lobster, your majesty?
  Scots kail brose or broth?
Grilled mackerel with gooseberry sauce?
  Cider ice that melts in your mouth?
Pears filled with nut and date salad?
  Christmas pudding with a tanner or a bob in?
Take it all away! groused the old King of Cornwall.
    Bring me some figgie hobbin!

Amber jelly, your majesty?
  Passion fruit flummery?
Pineapple sherbet, milk punch or Pavlova cake,
  Sugary, summery?
Carpet-bag steak, blueberry grunt, cinnamon crescents?
  Spaghetti as fine as the thread on a bobbin?
Take it all away! grizzled the old King of Cornwall.
    Bring me some figgie hobbin!

So in from the kitchen came figgie hobbin,
  Shining and speckled with raisins sweet,
And though on the King of Cornwall's land
  The rain it fell and the wind it beat,
As soon as a forkful of figgie hobbin
  Up to his lips he drew,
Over the palace a pure sun shone
  And the sky was blue.
THAT'S what I wanted! he smiled, his face
  Now as bright as the breast of the robin.
To cure the sickness of the heart, ah –
  Bring me some figgie hobbin!

THE REVEREND
SABINE BARING-GOULD

The Reverend Sabine Baring-Gould,
    Rector (sometime) at Lew,
Once at a Christmas party asked,
    'Whose pretty child are you?'

(The Rector's family was long,
    His memory was poor,
And as to who was who had grown
    Increasingly unsure).

At this, the infant on the stair
    Most sorrowfully sighed.
'Whose pretty little girl am I?
    Why, *yours*, papa!' she cried.

The Reverend Sabine Baring-Gould (1834–1924) was Rector for 43 years c
Lewtrenchard in Devon. He is the author of the hymn 'Onward, Christian soldiers'.

JOHNNIE GROAT SAYS

Johnnie Groat says my eyes are blue,
He says my hair is curled,
He says I am the prettiest maid
He saw in all the world.

Dearest, your hair is straight as string,
One eye is black, one brown,
And you are the homeliest-looking girl
Was ever in Launceston town.

Johnnie Groat says I'm smart and slim,
My hands are soft as snow,
And nobody walks as well as I
When to the fields I go.

Sweetheart, your shift is all in rags,
Your hands are red as kale,
And it's well-known at sixteen stone
You turn the miller's scale.

Johnnie Groat says my voice is sweet
As water is or wine,
And when my grannie goes up to heaven
Her pig and cot are mine.

Dear, when you walk about the wood
The birds fall down on the floor,
And your grannie of fifty years is good
For half a century more.

Then shall I not marry good Johnnie Groat
Who thinks so well of me?
And shall he not give me a fine gold ring
When he goes back to sea?

Daughter, but take the fine gold ring
And the love that's in his eye,
For the love that comes from an honest poor man
Is more than money can buy,
More than money can buy.

I TOOK MY
WIFE TO MARKET

I took my wife to market,
   It was not market day.
We had a hundred hens' eggs
   That never a fowl did lay.

We rode there in a trap, sir,
   Had neither wheel nor brake,
And from the yellow stable
   The pony did not take.

When we got to the market
   It was the crack of noon,
High in the tower the hooting owl
   And in the sky the moon.

And when we sold the eggs, sir,
   For neither coin nor gear,
We went into an ale-house
   That sold not wine nor beer.

We sat down by the church-yard
   When to eat we were fain.
The cheese it was not made of milk,
   Nor the bread from grain.

And when the fair was over
   We made our homeward way,
Deep in the west the dying moon
   And in the east the day.

I opened up my door, sir,
  No latch nor key had I,
And as we went downstairs to bed
  I heard the cockerel cry.

Although for years a thousand
  Upon this earth I be,
I want not such a day again
  For all the Queen's fee.

And though for years a thousand
  On earth I may grow old
I want not such a day again
  For all the King's gold.

GREEN MAN, BLUE MAN

As I was walking through Guildhall Square
I smiled to see a green man there,
But when I saw him coming near
My heart was filled with nameless fear.

As I was walking through Madford Lane
A blue man stood there in the rain.
I asked him in by my front-door,
For I'd seen a blue man before.

As I was walking through Landlake Wood
A grey man in the forest stood,
But when he turned and said, 'Good day'
I shook my head and ran away.

As I was walking by Church Stile
A purple man spoke there a while.
I spoke to him because, you see,
A purple man once lived by me.

But when the night falls dark and fell
How, O how, am I to tell,
Grey man, green man, purple, blue,
Which is which is which of you?

OLD MRS THING-UM-E-BOB

Old Mrs Thing-um-e-bob,
   Lives at you-know-where,
Dropped her what-you-may-call-it down
   The well of the kitchen stair.

'Gracious me!' said Thing-um-e-bob,
   'This don't look too bright.
I'll ask old Mr What's-his-name
   To try and put it right.'

Along came Mr What's-his-name,
   He said, 'You've broke the lot!
I'll have to see what I can do
   With some of the you-know-what.'

So he gave the what-you-may-call-it a pit
   And he gave it a bit of a pat,
And he put it all together again
   With a little of this and that.

And he gave the what-you-may-call-it a dib
   And he gave it a dab as well
When all of a sudden he heard a note
   As clear as any bell.

'It's as good as new!' cried What's-his-name.
   'But please remember, now,
In future Mrs Thing-um-e-bob
   You'll have to go you-know-how.'

IF YOU SHOULD
GO TO CAISTOR TOWN

If you should go to Caistor town
  Where my true-love has gone,
Ask her why she went away
  And left me here alone.

She said the Caistor sky was blue,
  The wind was never cold,
The pavements were all made of pearl,
  The young were never old.

Never a word she told me more
  But when the year was fled,
Upon a bed of brightest earth
  She laid her gentle head.

When I went up to Caistor
  My suit was made of black,
And all her words like summer birds
  Upon the air came back.

O when I went to Caistor
  With ice the sky was sown,
And all the streets were chill and grey
  And they were made of stone.

AT NINE OF THE NIGHT
I OPENED MY DOOR

At nine of the night I opened my door
That stands midway between moor and moor,
And all around me, silver-bright,
I saw that the world had turned to white.

Thick was the snow on field and hedge
And vanished was the river-sedge,
Where winter skilfully had wound
A shining scarf without a sound.

And as I stood and gazed my fill
A stable-boy came down the hill.
With every step I saw him take
Flew at his heel a puff of flake.

His brow was whiter than the hoar,
A beard of freshest snow he wore,
And round about him, snowflake starred,
A red horse-blanket from the yard.

In a red cloak I saw him go,
His back was bent, his step was slow,
And as he laboured through the cold
He seemed a hundred winters old.

I stood and watched the snowy head,
The whiskers white, the cloak of red.
'A Merry Christmas!' I heard him cry.
'The same to you, old friend,' said I.

TELL ME, TELL ME, SARAH JANE

Tell me, tell me, Sarah Jane,
  Tell me, dearest daughter,
Why are you holding in your hand
  A thimbleful of water?
Why do you hold it to your eye
  And gaze both late and soon
From early morning light until
  The rising of the moon?

Mother, I hear the mermaids cry,
  I hear the mermen sing,
And I can see the sailing-ships
  All made of sticks and string.
And I can see the jumping fish,
  The whales that fall and rise
And swim about the waterspout
  That swarms up to the skies.

Tell me, tell me, Sarah Jane,
  Tell your darling mother,
Why do you walk beside the tide
  As though you loved none other?
Why do you listen to a shell
  And watch the billows curl,
And throw away your diamond ring
  And wear instead the pearl?

Mother I hear the water
  Beneath the headland pinned,
And I can see the sea-gull
  Sliding down the wind.
I taste the salt upon my tongue
  As sweet as sweet can be.

Tell me, my dear, whose voice you hear?

It is the sea, the sea.

KING FOO FOO

King Foo Foo sat upon his throne
Dressed in his royal closes,
While all around his courtiers stood
With clothes-pegs on their noses.

'This action strange,' King Foo Foo said,
'My mind quie discomposes,
Though vulgar curiosity
A good king never shoses.'

But to the court it was as clear
As poetry or prose is:
King Foo Foo had not had a bath
Since goodness only knoses.

Till one fine day the Fire Brigade
Rehearsing with their hoses
(To Handel's 'Water Music' played
With many puffs and bloses)

Quite failed the water to control
In all its ebbs and floses
And simply drenched the King with sev-
Eral thousand gallon doses.

At this each wight (though impolite)
A mighty grin exposes.
'At last,' the King said, 'now I see
That all my court morose is!

'A debt to keep his courtiers gay
A monarch surely oweses,
And deep within my royal breast
A sporting heart reposes.'

So now each night its water bright
The Fire Brigade disposes
Over a King who smiles as sweet
As all the royal roses.

AT CANDLEMAS

'If Candlemas be fine and clear
There'll be two winters in that year';

But all the day the drumming sun
Brazened it out that spring had come,

And the tall elder on the scene
Unfolded the first leaves of green.

But when another morning came
With frost, as Candlemas with flame,

The sky was steel, there was no sun,
The elder leaves were dead and gone.

Out of a cold and crusted eye
The stiff pond stared up at the sky,

And on the scarcely-breathing earth
A killing wind fell from the north;

But still within the elder tree
The strong sap rose, though none
  could see.

TOM BONE

My name is Tom Bone,
I live all alone
In a deep house on Winter Street.
  Through my mud wall
  The wolf-spiders crawl
  And the mole has his beat.

On my roof of green grass
All the day footsteps pass
In the heat and the cold,
  As snug in a bed
  With my name at its head
  One great secret I hold.

Tom Bone, when the owls rise
In the drifting night skies
Do you walk round about?
  All the solemn hours through
  I lie down just like you
  And sleep the night out.

Tom Bone, as you lie there
On your pillow of hair,
What grave thoughts do you keep?
  Tom says, Nonsense and stuff!
  You'll know soon enough.
  Sleep, darling, sleep.

RAMHEAD AND DODMAN

Said Ramhead to Dodman
  As proudly they stood
Their brows in the heavens
  Their feet in the flood,

'Of all the tall headlands
  That hold back the sea
Throughout Cornwall's kingdom,
  The greatest is me!'

Said Dodman to Ramhead,
  'Of all cliff-tops high
The stoutest, the strongest,
  The sturdiest am I!

'And never O never
  In cold or in heat
Old Ramhead and Dodman
  Together will meet.'

But softly the sea
  As they chanted their rhyme
Said, 'I'll swallow the pair of you
  All in good time.

'For deep in my belly
    There's room and to spare,
And I promise you both
    A safe meeting down there,

'Where mother nor father
    Nor sister nor brother
Will Ramhead and Dodman
    Tell one from the other,

'Though Dodman and Ramhead
    Today you may stand
Your heads in the heavens,
    Your feet on the sand.'

*The Cornish saying 'When Ramhead and Dodman meet' means 'never'. Rame Head
rmerly known as Ramhead) and Dodman are headlands, twenty-five miles apart, in
th Cornwall.*

COLONEL FAZACKERLEY

Colonel Fazackerley Butterworth-Toast
Bought an old castle complete with a ghost,
But someone or other forgot to declare
To Colonel Fazack that the spectre was there.

On the very first evening, while waiting to dine,
The Colonel was taking a fine sherry wine,
When the ghost, with a furious flash and a flare,
Shot out of the chimney and shivered, 'Beware!'

Colonel Fazackerley put down his glass
And said, 'My dear fellow, that's really first class!
I just can't conceive how you do it at all.
I imagine you're going to a Fancy Dress Ball?'

At this, the dread ghost gave a withering cry.
Said the Colonel (his monocle firm in his eye),
'Now just how you do it I wish I could think.
Do sit down and tell me, and please have a drink.'

The ghost in his phosphorous cloak gave a roar
And floated about between ceiling and floor.
He walked through a wall and returned through a pa
And backed up the chimney and came down again.

Said the Colonel, 'With laughter I'm feeling quite wea
(As trickles of merriment ran down his cheek).
'My house-warming party I hope you won't spurn.
You *must* say you'll come and you'll give us a turn!'

At this, the poor spectre – quite out of his wits –
Proceeded to shake himself almost to bits.
He rattled his chains and he clattered his bones
And he filled the whole castle with mumbles and moans

But Colonel Fazackerley, just as before,
Was simply delighted and called out, 'Encore!'
At which the ghost vanished, his efforts in vain,
And never was seen at the castle again.

'Oh dear, what a pity!' said Colonel Fazack.
'I don't know his name, so I can't call him back.'
And then with a smile that was hard to define,
Colonel Fazackerley went in to dine.

MY YOUNG MAN'S
A CORNISHMAN

My young man's a Cornishman
He lives in Camborne town,
I met him going up the hill
As I was coming down.

His eye is bright as Dolcoath tin,
His body as china clay,
His hair is dark as Werrington Wood
Upon St Thomas's Day.

He plays the rugby football game
On Saturday afternoon,
And we shall walk on Wilsey Down
Under the bouncing moon.

My young man's a Cornishman,
Won't leave me in the lurch,
And one day we shall married be
Up to Trura church.   *Truro Cathedral*

He's bought me a ring of Cornish gold,
A belt of copper made,
At Bodmin Fair for my wedding-dress
A purse of silver paid.

And I shall give him scalded cream
And starry-gazy pie,
And make him a saffron cake for tea
And a pasty for by and by.

My young man's a Cornishman,
A proper young man is he,
And a Cornish man with a Cornish maid
Is how it belongs to be.

A starry-gaze pie is a fish pie, made of pilchards. The fish are cooked whole, with heads piercing the crust as though gazing up to the heavens.

AS I WENT
DOWN THE CAT-WALK

As I went down the cat-walk
    Where all the catkins blow,
I saw an old cat-burglar
    Beside a cattalo*.
And O he miaowed and O he mewed
    Just like the cat-bird's call.
I said, 'Pray cease this catalogue
    Of scatty caterwaul.
I didn't catch your name, I fear,
    But how, my dear old chap,
Among such cataracts of tears
    May I take my cat-nap?'

He said, 'Of various cat-calls
   I'm running the gamut
Because upon my cat-fish
   No catsup has been put!
Such catchpenny behaviour
   It makes me ill, then iller.'
I said, 'Please don't excite yourself.
   Lean on this caterpillar.'
I plucked from off the apple tree
   A juicy, ripe cat's-head.
He took it with some cat-lap
   And felt much better fed.
And then he played cat's-cradle
   And turned cat in the pan,
And sailed to Catalonia
   All in a catamaran.
He sailed away by Catalan Bay†
   That happy cataman.

* A cross between a buffalo and a cow.
† In Gibraltar.

A SAILOR SAT
ON THE WATERY SHORE

A sailor sat on the watery shore
    By the side of the shiny sea,
And as the billows railed and roared
    These words he said to me.
'I've sailed to the Rock from Plymouth Dock
    And from Sydney to Simonstown,
And oh but it's true that a life on the blue
    Ain't the same as the life on the brown.

For there's gusts and there's gales and there's
    spirting whales
  And there's fish flying round like a fountain,
And there's bays and there's bights and there's
    Great Northern Lights,
  And there's oceans as deep as a mountain.
And then there's your mates in the varying states
  From the angel and saint to the sinner,
Though I think you will find they are much of a kind
  When you sit down beside 'em for dinner.

'And yarns by the fathom you'll hear 'em all spin
    Of ghost-ships and sea-serpents mighty,
Of mermaids divine, and of Crossing the Line
    With King Neptune and Queen Amphitrite.
O many the lays I could sing of the days
    As in suits dazzling white from the dhoby   *the was*
We sauntered ashore in New York, Singapore,
    Or went up the line to Nairobi.

'And your eyes, my young friend, would jump out of
        your head,
    When the ship bade old England good-bye-ee,
At the antics of tars to the sound of guitars
    Whether strummed in Cadiz or Hawaii.
You may search the world through, but no friend is
        true
    As the matelot so gay and stout-hearted,
Though when he comes on leave (and to tell it, I griev
    There's no man from his pay sooner parted.

'Furthermore,' said the sailor, 'it's certain to me
    As this beach is all covered with sand,
Though a sailor may find many sharks in the sea
    He will find even more on the land.'
'Ah sailor,' I said, 'but I feel that your heart
    For the world of the wave is still yearning,
And I think I surmise from the look in your eyes
    That to it you'll soon be returning.'

ood gracious!' the sailor said. 'Certainly not,
And I can't think what gave you the notion
at once having left it, I'd wish to return
To the dark, unpredictable ocean.
e a nice little semi in Citadel Road
That faces away from the sea,
d the reason it's thus – but, dear me, there's my bus
And it's time for my afternoon tea!'

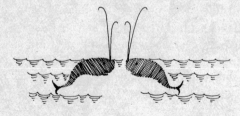

LOGS OF WOOD

When in the summer sky the sun
Hung like a golden ball,
John Willy from the Workhouse came
And loudly he would bawl:

Wood! Wood! Logs of wood
To keep out the cold!
Shan't be round tomorrow!
They all must be sold!

But O the sky was shining blue
And green was the spray.
It seemed as if the easy days
Would never pass away.

And when John Willy came to town
The laughter it would start,
And we would smile as he went by
Pushing his wooden cart.

John Willy, I can see you still,
Coming down Tower Street,
Your pointed nose, your cast-off clothes,
Your Charlie Chaplin feet.

And like the prophet you would stand
Calling loud and long,
But there were few who listened to
The story of your song.

Wood! Wood! Logs of wood
To keep out the cold!
Shan't be round tomorrow!
They all must be sold!

But now the snow is on the hill,
The ice is on the plain,
And dark as dark a shadow falls
Across my window-pane.

Tomorrow, ah, tomorrow –
That name I did not fear
Until Tomorrow came and said,
Good morrow. I am here.

IN THE
WILLOW GARDENS

In the Willow Gardens
Where once was wood and brake
A hundred town allotments
Come down to Harper's Lake.
In the Willow Gardens
Under the castle keep
A hundred town allotments
Stand beside the steep.

And here Tom tends his cabbage plants
And digs his taters out,
And leans upon a smudgy spade
To watch his Brussels sprout;
And brother Jack spreads chicken wire
For fear the fowls should stray,
And nails up bits of galvanized
To keep the wind away.

But in the Willow Gardens
I don't hear Tom nor Jack,
But I can hear the huntsmen
Along the forest track.
All through the Willow Gardens
I see them riding plain,
The iron knights of Normandy
And Robert of Mortain.

They ride along by Harper's Lake
Beside the water clear;
They hunt the hare, they hunt the boar,
They hunt the running deer.
Hark, I hear the hoof-beats,
I hear the hunters cry,
I hear them blow the hunting-horn,
I see the arrows fly!

'Don't you see them, Tommy,
And don't you see them, Jack?
And how they ride by the stream-side
To the wood's end and back?'

But Tommy shakes his silver head
And Jackie slaps his knee.
'There's nothing here,' says Jack to Tom.
'Maze as a brush!' says he.   *crazy*

And Tommy goes on digging,
And Jackie bangs a nail.
'Better go home,' they say to me.
'You'm looking wisht and pale.'   *unwell*
But still I see the huntsmen
Riding low and high
As plain as I see Jack and Tom.
I do not tell a lie.

ONE DAY AT
A PERRANPORTH PET-SHOP

One day at a Perranporth pet-shop
  On a rather wild morning in June,
A lady from Par bought a budgerigar
  And she sang to a curious tune:
'Say that you love me, my sweetheart,
  My darling, my dovey, my pride,
My very own jewel, my dear one!'
  'Oh lumme,' the budgie replied.

'I'll feed you entirely on cream-cakes
  And doughnuts all smothered in jam,
And puddings and pies of incredible size,
  And peaches and melons and ham.
And you shall drink whiskies and sodas,
  For comfort your cage shall be famed.
You shall sleep in a bed lined with satin.'
  'Oh crikey!' the budgie exclaimed.

But the lady appeared not to hear him
  For she showed neither sorrow nor rage,
As with common-sense tardy and action foolhardy
  She opened the door of his cage.
'Come perch on my finger, my honey,
  To show you are mine, O my sweet!' –
Whereupon the poor fowl with a shriek and a howl
  Took off like a jet down the street.

And high he flew up above Cornwall
  To ensure his escape was no failure,
Then his speed he increased and he flew south and east
  To his ancestral home in Australia.
For although to the Australian abo
  The word 'budgerigar' means 'good food',
He said, 'I declare I'll feel much safer there
  Than in Bodmin or Bugle or Bude.'

ENVOI

And I'm sure with the budgie's conclusion
  You all will agree without fail:
Best eat frugal and free in a far-distant tree
  Than down all the wrong diet in jail.

THE MERRYMAID

Robert Stephen Hawker,
Vicar of Morwenstow,
Dressed himself in a merrymaid skin,
Swam out with the flow.

And with a coral-branch he combed
His hair so limp and long,
And high in a screamy voice he sang
A sea-weedy sort of song.

From near and far the people came
To walk on the cliff-top green,
For none had heard a merrymaid sing
Nor ever a merrymaid seen.

The first night that the merrymaid sang
The moon was white as bone,
And sad was the song they heard her sing
As she sat on a slippery stone.

The second night that the merrymaid sang
The moon was beaming brass,
And sweet was the song they heard her sing
As she gazed in her looking-glass.

The third night that the merrymaid sang
The moon was thin and pale,
And when she had sung her sweet-sad song
She stood up straight on her tail.

As stiff as a soldier she stood up
In a phosphorescent sheen,
And with arms straight down by her sides she sang
'God Save our Gracious Queen.'

Then into the dancing sea she dove
To the running billows' roar,
And vanished beneath the wheeling waves
And was seen on the coast no more.

Robert Stephen Hawker,
Vicar of Morwenstow,
Stripped himself of the merrymaid skin
He wore from top to toe.

And the Vicar he smiled and pondered
As he went upstairs to bed
On the gullibility of man,
And sadly he shook his head.

*In Cornwall, a mermaid is called
a merrymaid. The poet
Robert Stephen Hawker (1803–75)
was Vicar of Morwenstow,
on the north coast of Cornwall,
from 1834. His best-known ballad is
'And shall Trelawny die?'.*

LORD LOVELACE

Lord Lovelace rode home from the wars,
His wounds were black as ice,
While overhead the winter sun
Hung out its pale device.

The lance was tattered in his hand,
Sundered his axe and blade,
And in a bloody coat of war
Lord Lovelace was arrayed.

And he was sick and he was sore
But never sad was he,
And whistled bright as any bird
Upon an April tree.

'Soon, soon,' he cried, 'at Lovelace Hall
Fair Ellen I shall greet,
And she with loving heart and hand
Will make my sharp wounds sweet.

'And Young Jehan the serving-man
Will bring the wine and bread,
And with a yellow link will light
Us to the bridal bed.'

But when he got to Lovelace Hall
Burned were both wall and stack,
And in the stinking moat the tower
Had tumbled on its back.

And none welcomed Lord Lovelace home
Within the castle shell,
And ravaged was the land about
That Lord Lovelace knew well.

Long in his stirrups Lovelace stood
Before his broken door,
And slowly rode he down the hill
Back to the bitter war.

Nor mercy showed he from that day,
Nor tear fell from his eye,
And rich and poor both fearful were
When Black Lovelace rode by.

This tale is true that now I tell
To woman and to man,
As Fair Ellen is my wife's name
And mine is Young Jehan.

MY NEIGHBOUR
MR NORMANTON

My neighbour Mr Normanton
Who lives at ninety-five
'S as typical an Englishman
As any one alive.

He wears pin-stripes and bowler-hat.
His accent is sublime.
He keeps a British bull-dog
And British Summer Time.

His shoes are always glassy black
(He never wears the brown);
His brolly's rolled slim as a stick
When he goes up to town.

He much prefers a game of darts
To mah-jongg or to chess.
He fancies Chelsea for the Cup
And dotes on G. & S.

Roast beef and Yorkshire pudding are
What he most likes to eat.
His drinks are tea and British beer
And sometimes whisky (neat).

Out of a British briar-pipe
He puffs an Empire smoke
While gazing at his roses (red)
Beneath a British oak.

And in his British garden
Upon St George's Day
He hoists a British Union Jack
And shouts, 'Hip, hip, hooray!'

But tell me, Mr Normanton,
That evening after dark,
Who were those foreign gentlemen
You met in Churchill Park?

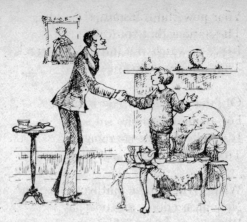

You spoke a funny language
I couldn't understand;
And wasn't that some microfilm
You'd hidden in your hand?

And then that note I saw you post
Inside a hollow tree!
When I jumped out you turned about
As quick as quick could be.

Why did you use a hearing-aid
While strolling in the park
And talking to that worried-looking
Admiralty clerk?

The day you took the cypher-book
From underneath a stone,
I'm certain, Mr Normanton,
You thought you were alone.

Your powerful transmitter!
The stations that you call!
I love to watch you through the crack
That's in my bedroom wall.

Oh, thank you, Mr Normanton,
For asking me to tea.
It's really all quite riveting
To clever chaps like me.

What? Will I come and work for you?
Now please don't mention pay.
What super luck I left a note
To say I'd run away!

Is that a gun that's in your hand?
And look! A lethal pill!
And that's a real commando-knife?
I say, this is a thrill!

Of course I've never said a word
About the things you do.
Let's keep it all a secret
Between just me and . . .

77

BILLY MEDALS

Do you know Billy Medals
That warrior bold,
His stars made of silver,
His circles of gold?
O there don't seem a battle
Of land, sea or air
For fifty years past
But old Bill wasn't there.

He stands on the corner
As straight as a gun,
And his circles and stars
Catch the rays of the sun.
His stars and his circles
All glitter and gleam,
And just like the rainbow
His ribbons they beam.

You must know Billy Medals
With his chestful of gongs,
He knows all the war-stories
And all the war-songs.
His jacket is ragged
His trousers are green,
And no one stands straighter
For 'God Save the Queen'.

Around his torn topper
Are badges in scores
Of goodness knows how many
Different corps.
But in war Billy Medals
Has never known harm
For he's never been farther
Than Fiveacre Farm.

When lads from the village
Dodged shrapnel and shell,
Billy Medals was cleaning out
Wishworthy Well.
When in deserts they sweated,
In oceans they froze,
Billy Medals was scaring
The rooks and the crows.

Did you see the brave soldier
New-home from the war
Give Billy the star
That once proudly he bore?
Billy Medals he cackled
And capered with glee
And the village-boys laughed,
But the soldier, not he.

MILLER'S END

When we moved to Miller's End,
   Every afternoon at four
A thin shadow of a shade
   Quavered through the garden-door.

Dressed in black from top to toe
   And a veil about her head
To us all it seemed as though
   She came walking from the dead.

With a basket on her arm
   Through the hedge-gap she would pass,
Never a mark that we could spy
   On the flagstones or the grass.

When we told the garden-boy
   How we saw the phantom glide,
With a grin his face was bright
   As the pool he stood beside.

'That's no ghost-walk,' Billy said,
   'Nor a ghost you fear to stop –
Only old Miss Wickerby
   On a short cut to the shop.'

So next day we lay in wait,
   Passed a civil time of day,
Said how pleased we were she came
   Daily down our garden-way.

Suddenly her cheek it paled,
    Turned, as quick, from ice to flame.
'Tell me,' said Miss Wickerby.
    'Who spoke of me, and my name?'

'Bill the garden-boy.'
                            She sighed,
    Said, 'Of course, you could not know
How he drowned – that very pool –
    A frozen winter – long ago.'

A DAY IN EARLY SUMMER

A day in early summer
The first year of the war,
Davy Jones and I sat down
By the North Sea-shore.

The sun was bright, warm was the sand,
The sky was hot and blue.
How long we sat there
I never knew:

Rigged in brand-new uniforms,
Two naval sprogs
Dozing in the dancing sun,
Tired as dogs.

Suddenly a child's voice spoke
Across the silent shore:
'Look at those two sailors!
I wonder who they are?'

I sat up and looked about
The yellow and the blue
For the sailors on the shore.
I wondered, too.

Not a seaman could I see
As far as sight could reach:
Only the locked-up pier, the rolls
Of barbed-wire on the beach;

Only the tank-traps on the prom
By the shallow bay;
A woman and a little child
Wandering away;

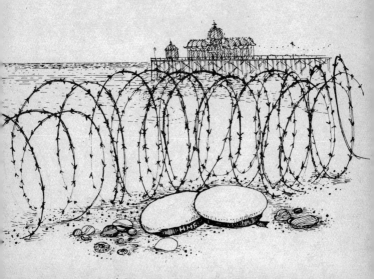

Only Davy Jones and I
Wearing tiddley suits,
Lanyards, caps with 'HMS',
Shiny pussers' boots.   *naval issue*

Gold help England, then I thought,
Gazing out to sea,
If all between it and the foe
Is Davy Jones, and me.

MARY, MARY MAGDALENE

On the east wall of the church of St Mary Magdalene at Launceston in Cornwall is a granite figure of the saint. The children of the town say that a stone lodged on her back will bring good luck.

Mary, Mary Magdalene
Lying on the wall,
I throw a pebble on your back.
Will it lie or fall?

Send me down for Christmas
Some stockings and some hose,
And send before the winter's end
A brand-new suit of clothes.

Mary, Mary Magdalene
Under a stony tree,
I throw a pebble on your back.
What will you send me?

I'll send you for your Christening
A woollen robe to wear,
A shiny cup from which to sup,
And a name to bear.

Mary, Mary Magdalene
Lying cool as snow,
What will you be sending me
When to school I go?

I'll send a pencil and a pen
That write both clean and neat.
And I'll send to the schoolmaster
A tongue that's kind and sweet.

Mary, Mary Magdalene
Lying in the sun,
What will you be sending me
Now I'm twenty-one?

I'll send you down a locket
As silver as your skin,
And I'll send you a lover
To fit a gold key in.

Mary, Mary Magdalene
Underneath the spray,
What will you be sending me
On my wedding-day?

I'll send you down some blossom,
Some ribbons and some lace,
And for the bride a veil to hide
The blushes on her face.

Mary, Mary Magdalene
Whiter than the swan,
Tell me what you'll send me,
Now my good man's dead and gone.

I'll send to you a single bed
On which you must lie,
And pillows bright where tears may light
That fall from your eye.

Mary, Mary Magdalene
Now nine months are done,
What will you be sending me
For my little son?

I'll send you for your baby
A lucky stone, and small,
To throw to Mary Magdalene
Lying on the wall.

SIR FREDERICK

Stiffly Sir Frederick
Stumps the green cobble-stones,
Opens the gate
By the stable door,
Hums as he strolls
In the pale of the afternoon
A faded old song
Of the First World War.

He lifts up his feet
Like a stork by the river bed,
Treads the long grass
Where the narcissi lean,
Plucks perhaps six or seven,
And at a sting-nettle
Strikes with his infantry-
Officer's cane.

Then in the library
Of his great mansion,
Books at attention
On every shelf,
Shakily signs his name
In his biography,
Serves tea and Dundee cake,
Has some himself.

Just as I drive away
I catch a glimpse of him
Dodging as best he can
Bullets of rain,
And as a thunder-clap
Bursts like a howitzer
He melts in the history-
Books once again.

ROUND THE TOWN

Round the town with Billy,
  Round the town with Sue,
  From Sunday morning to Saturday night
  With nothing else to do.

What do you do on Monday?
  We look up at the sky
  Waiting for a drying wind
  To make the washing fly.

What do you do on Tuesday?
  From underneath the stair
  We see them take the wooden horse
  To let the linen air.

What do you do on Wednesday?
  We watch the butchers' men
  Drive the frightened animals
  In and out the pen.

What do you do on Thursday?
  On early-closing day
  We see the shops are safely locked
  And the money put away.

What do you do on Friday?
  The local paper's read
  To find if we are still alive
  Or whether we are dead.

What do you do on Saturday?
    We sit and hold our breath
    And see the silver cowboys
    Shoot themselves to death.

What do you do on Sunday?
    We listen for the bell
    And pray to Christ our Saviour
    To guard and keep us well.

What do you do on Monday?
    We look out through the pane
    And if it's wet or if it's fine
    Begin all over again.

MY MOTHER
SAW A DANCING BEAR

My mother saw a dancing bear
By the schoolyard, a day in June.
The keeper stood with chain and bar
And whistle-pipe, and played a tune.

And bruin lifted up its head
And lifted up its dusty feet,
And all the children laughed to see
It caper in the summer heat.

They watched as for the Queen it died.
They watched it march. They watched it halt.
They heard the keeper as he cried,
'Now, roly-poly!' 'Somersault!'

And then, my mother said, there came
The keeper with a begging-cup,
The bear with burning coat of fur,
Shaming the laughter to a stop.

They paid a penny for the dance,
But what they saw was not the show;
Only, in bruin's aching eyes,
Far-distant forests, and the snow.

WHO?

Who is that child I see wandering, wandering
Down by the side of the quivering stream?
Why does he seem not to hear, though I call to him
Where does he come from, and what is his name?

Why do I see him at sunrise and sunset
Taking, in old-fashioned clothes, the same track?
Why, when he walks, does he cast not a shadow
Though the sun rises and falls at his back?

Why does the dust lie so thick on the hedgerow
By the great field where a horse pulls the plough?
Why do I see only meadows, where houses
Stand in a line by the riverside now?

Why does he move like a wraith by the water,
Soft as the thistledown on the breeze blown?
When I draw near him so that I may hear him,
Why does he say that his name is my own?